After Pyre

P.M. Draper

A Publication of The Poetry Box®

Poems ©2022 P.M. Draper
All rights reserved.

Editing & Book Layout: Shawn Aveningo Sanders
Cover Art & Design: Robert R. Sanders
Author Photo: Michael Gallagher

No part of this book may be reproduced in any manner whatsoever without permission from the author, except in the case of brief quotations embodied in critical essays, reviews and articles.

ISBN: 978-1-956285-20-8
Printed in the United States of America.
Wholesale Distribution via Ingram.

Published by The Poetry Box®, September 2022
Portland, Oregon
ThePoetryBox.com

To Sally, for showing me the way

Contents

9	Illuminati
10	A Time Like This
11	I Come
12	Gulls • *Los Rifles* • *Valparaiso* • Bakery
13	Requiem
14	The Meaning of Thanks
15	Touch
16	*And That's The Way It Is*, Mr.Cronkite
17	Baptism
18	Memory's Biscuits
19	Primary Colors
21	Tribe
22	Cousin, Interrupted
23	Pyre, I-V
28	A Field Guide to Crazy
29	Trio
30	Ancestry
31	*Carpe Diem* Meets Nana on Hollywood Blvd.
32	Elemental
33	Table for One
34	More Likely than Watching Squirrel Sex
35	Kung Fu Nuns of Kathmandu
36	Lawrence Ferlinghetti Says Goodbye
37	From My Caesura

39	Acknowledgments
41	Praise for *After Pyre*
43	About the Author

Our dreams have been assaulted by a memory that will not sleep.

—William Carlos Williams

Illuminati

The five AM train whistle echoes hollow, in the last of night.
I ponder what the pastry's like in Amsterdam.
Is the coffee really Viennese?
Wanderlust teases as I bend down to feed the ferals at the gate.
A full spring moon spotlights the sky:

Illuminati, black and white, mosaic street corners trick my eyes
shadows playing hide the night.
I still live by the clock, but the day approaches when I'll not.
Now, I'll wonder what's for breakfast in Bangkok,
tending work and home front in quarantine.

O, Patagonia!
Your syllables invite me to a land under
through Tierra del Fuego.

If Magellan only knew, the Pacific wasn't half of the story.
Pigafetta set the Spanish king straight,
once the liars left the court.

All for spice. Siren song of those islands,
that maiden voyage 'round the world.
A Portuguese captain stricken
before the arc of destiny.

A Time Like This

I never want to forget
those twenty-six hours
you last came home—

The soft knock on my bedroom door
at five in the morning
jumping on my bed,
sprawled across the foot
telling stories of Baghdad and beyond
as I sipped coffee.

The clock stood still.

Social-distancing be damned—
You're my sugar-bear, my youngest,
even at thirty-two, these hugs can't wait
another three months
until I see you again.

I'll always take my chances with you

as we climb into the rental Mustang
revving the engine, ready for a spin.

I Come

from Chautauqua, it's 'Shawtawqua' (in Iroquois)
meaning bag-tied-in-the-middle, like the shape of our lake.
or Chautauqua Institution, a tradition of summer.

Western New York rural: land of Holsteins and Appaloosas,
grown big on the farms, Concord vines on the hillsides.
If you know how to cast, Walleye and Muskelunge
are the lure of Chautauqua's water.

Sweet corn, husked before dinner, slathered
hot with butter, spells delicious with roast beef on 'wicks,
spread with horseradish. Dessert means rhubarb, mouth-
puckering pie loaded with strawberries, or Dog-in-Suds
drive-in root beer floats, with Dylan rolling on the radio.

Boys snicker about snipe hunting and girls sneak cigarettes.
Lovers' Lane steaming as muscle cars cruise 17J.
Fireflies at twilight mean summertime, hot time with John
Sebastian and the Lovin' Spoonful, or whatever's on CK-101
out of Detroit.

Yeah, I was one of the locals. Not one of the summer people
with wallets out, noses up while they talk over
at the Institute. Dear Gawd, no. I stayed.
Went to school, worked my job and prayed for a way out
after snowstorms in May.

Gulls • *Los Rifles* • *Valparaiso* • Bakery

I don't want to go back to tear gas and riots—
police on every corner, shouldering *los rifles*
and endless lines for rations of cooking oil, toilet paper.
You can have my share.

I'll wait for the all-clear and take
the afternoon train to *Vina del Mar* and catch the local,
the bus to *Valparaiso*,
the coastal that rides along the beach.

Ocean pungent air grabs your nostrils
while the gulls cry and the smell of oven-ready bread
wafts from the corner bakery.

Horns blare when the earth trembles
in Chile, even after forty-eight years.
Welcome back, gringa.

Requiem

He said te amo, my little gringa.
He said I was the light of his life,
that he loved me.
He said so much it frightened me.

I remember the thrill of those letters,
the feel of the onion-skin paper,
and how I loved reading what he wrote.
I remember the liquid timbre of his voice, quicksilver in his smile.

I didn't talk to anyone about him, but my sister would tease me.

I didn't know my heart's desire.   How could I possibly be his?

The Meaning of Thanks

Going home after an ER visit.

∞

Sipping hot steaming java on a Monday morning,
another day, together, virus-free.

∞

Savoring orchid blooms one more time
as they steal the blue sky
right in the middle of your smile.

Touch

Blush at the thought of
what our touch used to be.

Smile as the memory fills your mind.

Chiseled thighs tentacled through steamy nights.

Touch me again, let your fingers find still true
the spark of embers in our embrace, our delight.

Nestle with me now, flesh it out, and remember
caresses cradled pillow-soft, melting
into kisses that taste of forever.

No cancer will ever take that away.

It's not a spin on what we had,
but, a new direction   pioneered by survival.

Untouchable.

And That's the Way It Is, Mr. Cronkite

My Brownie uniform is laid out on the bed,
the television on, blaring the news in black and white.
Shouts everywhere of 1963, the President shot, dead.

And where's Mom?

The cocoa-colored dress is soft but sturdy
with metal troop numbers pinned,
double-sewn seams, to serve God and country.
That Girl Scout promise I believe in, pledge allegiance to
at seven. No egg monsters or sounds that scrape the night.

Yet, where are you, Mom?

The Queen of England is in my dreams
saying goodbye to Camelot.
Walter Cronkite monologues, his bass of a voice
unravels the unthinkable. The Yanks keep weeping.

The horse-drawn carriage with his coffin
inches by
as the Kennedy toddler salutes his father.
His mother stands sentinel.
Russians scheme post-Sputnik
while the Chinese build their rocket-prototype for Mars.

Mom, where are you?

Baptism

Half a century ago, hired out
at twelve to babysit for the summer,
a friend of my mother's needed help.

I remember feeling grown-up, proud,
thinking I was helping out.
I had a job, not realizing the price to be paid.

But the days were all the same.
I missed Kristie and Laura,
spending afternoons at the lake,
lazing hours away on the float.
Munching on the world's best crispy fries
slathered in ketchup, as we giggled about stares
from funny-looking boys we didn't know.

I don't remember the kids or their mother,
but watching All My Children, Hollywood Squares
and the trailer with floorboards
that gave when you walked
just like that other trailer when I was four
and strangers in suits came, bringing canned goods
in boxes for the divorced lady with four kids,
the newest member of the congregation.

Memory's Biscuits

Granny Goose-ma'am moves deliberate,
a limp-waddle in her walk.
She never questions why I come,
only smiles, wiping hands
on her dress of an apron,
biscuits baking in the wood-burning stove.

Questions clipped,
as her tongue tosses
the toothpick side to side,
an economy of words,
between wheezes,
and occasional spittle.

Coal black eyes give me the once-over,
Catch my leaky boots dripping
on the doormat, sock footprints trailing on the floor,
a button missing on my winter coat.

She never asks about the accident
or grills me with what-abouts,
but, laser-whips words out of me
I never knew were coming.

She ministers in silent servings
steaming biscuits, real butter
with homemade strawberry jam.

My steps creak on worn linoleum,
after hours spent in kitchen minutes.
When I go, she leaves the door
unlocked, knowing I'll be back,
to Cafe Granny Guzman.

Primary Colors

Charles Alfred Draper
of the John Birch Society,
believed in Ronald Reagan's America.
His framed letter on White House
stationery thanked him for his support.

The red-white-and-blue
starched into his beliefs
incorporated his ministry, his religion.
The New Testament guide
to life suited him, the Church of Christ style
in a black and white way.

The apostle Paul had it all sewn up
in a primer for living, for those married,
for subscribers to the faith.

One-two-three, yessirree, be baptized
and be saved, via GeezUS.

Can we get an Amen?

The salvation of the Lord can be yours
for one simple price: acquiesce, stay nice
and quiet if you're a girl.
That's right, no speaking in the church.
Don't even think
about playing the piano.

After ten years with Mom this dogma
must have been Dad's relief.
No more banshee wails,
or wondering what she's doing today
or where she's taken off, with four kids in tow.

Who am I to say what made their marriage fail?

[. . .]

On this road to Damascus, do what you're told:
forget the bold initiatives
to turn the tables, love thy neighbor
even those not in the church building.

Hellfire and brimstone beliefs trump
suggestions to consider:

What would Jesus do?

Get on your knees: Pray for the light
to see every single shade of a son's rainbow,
even when he has AIDS.

Tribe

First airplane trip at twelve, a sojourn south alone,
I land in Melbourne. Stepping out of the plane,
the June sun jolts with a furnace blast of air off the tarmac.
Every pore of skin opens up, sweat staining new clothes,
sticking to my thighs. Welcome to Florida.

I remember my mother's mother's words:
'be nice: Grandpa Earle has money, kiddo'
It always comes down to cash.

I'm reporting in, sharing edits of my life
that can be discussed with the hard of hearing.
Mom's head shaving and drinking will not be mentioned.
But how do I explain missing school for thirty-three days?

What will we talk about? He doesn't bring up
living in Washington, working
under Presidents Roosevelt or Truman.
I never think to ask.
He tells me about Norris, Tennesee
and their centennial celebration.
The framed newspaper article
features him, city planner.

I remember the graduate student interviewing him,
recording his words for the University of Georgia.

I don't recall his PhD on the wall until he dies.
But the poinsettias climbing towards the roof outside,
 catch my eye.

The stain of being Mary's kid blinds me.

Will it ever fade?

Cousin, Interrupted

Palsied moves of gnarled hands
reveal the truth of your age.

I remember you that day, a lifetime ago
out of college, on Vero's beach:
running zigzag back and forth,
tossing frisbee with me.

We laughed at the nothing
in everything, squeezing the pleasure
out of sand between toes
and cold salty tickling waves.

I wonder why there weren't more memories like this.

I was only visiting and visits meant plane trips
schedules, plans in advance.

Not spur of the moment in a glance
hey, cous', let's check out the water.

I can't imagine what your younger self would think
to see you like this,
in a place called LifeCare
where's there's more than a whiff
of what's right around the corner.

PYRE

I.

I wish I could shimmy like my sister Kate

A ragtime tune, my childhood theme song,
salute to Katherine Norma, my sister Kate.

Older, she was the gorgeous one,
with the dimpled cheerleader smile,
A sleek brunette with flashing black-brown eyes
that followed you everywhere. How she looked like
Coltrane blues before she knew what she was playing.

She had a laugh beyond her years
throaty, guttural.
She'd give a sidelong glance that said,
"watch me, kid: it's like this"
and off she'd walk, with a hint of a wiggle.

Then, Kate knew exactly what she was doing.
She drove the boys crazy-wild.

Pregnant, she married at sixteen.

[. . .]

II.

A baby at sixteen changes everything. The world's axis shifts in ways a teenager can never fathom. The future is redefined. Doors shut, focus narrows. Survival is day-to-day. Dreams are for others. Now, there's a baby. But babies grow and jobs provide. On a good day, enough. Weeks, months and then years pass. The future is here and Kate's survived. Sober. It's time to try on one of those dreams for size. Nursing school. She's accepted and studies harder than she has for anything else before. And, she's done it. She graduates valedictorian at age thirty-eight. The world is hers again.

Until it's not.

III.

It was a rite of passage, appeal of the forbidden:
Boone's Farm wine in brown paper bags
brought to teen-age parties at the pavilion,
purchased by older buddies after secret promises.

Kate told me once that it tasted like candy
when I asked her why she drank and drank daily.

She had pet names for liquor, Jingle Bells for J&B
that sounded cutesy, now pathetic.

A predilection, genetic that is simply straightforward
but then, heartbreaking in how it swallowed her.

Twelve steps gave her back her life
one day at a time, until the cravings surfaced again,
wanting more,
after the dance with depression.

In the company of divorce, the madness
overtook her. She thought she could handle it,
but there's no bargaining with the monster of addiction:

either killed or be killed.

[. . .]

IV.

A shot was fired. He had no doubt of what the sound was. The still of the cool autumn morning was interrupted by a harsh pop. He was sitting on his porch, drinking coffee. It was too early for deer season. What could it be? The next morning, he heard of the neighbor lady found outside her house, next to the garage. Next to the garbage cans, found burned to death. He sighed. She hadn't seemed depressed but he had to admit, he didn't really know her. She and her husband had just been together a few years. And, there was a son, too; hers, apparently. He didn't remember the last time he had been around. And, she was burned to death? I wonder what that shot was...

V.

I feel uncomfortable with the price
purists pay for their beliefs.
Buddist priests haven't made American news
since setting themselves on fire during Vietnam.
I cannot grasp what made them do it.

I cannot grasp what made you do it.
I don't accept the words printed
on the death certificate that read,
self-immolation, death by fire, at one's own hand.
Kate, somehow, I think you'd agree.

Remember how you told me about Chuck?
Mom couldn't do it. We mulled over how it happened,
time and time again. Car accident, explosion, fire.
Brother killed in less than a minute.

We'd comment on how he died
vowing, never. Never. As if teen-age words
would protect us from future's vagaries.

Sisters' pledge sealed in years, extinguished
in the amber of ashes.

A Field Guide to Crazy

Kate used to say that life with Mom was like a ping-pong ball in a hurricane. You never knew what was coming next or where you'd be going. No two days were alike. Yet she was my mother. In spite of everything, those urges to love or connect never went away. It just felt confusing, trying to reconcile emotion with everyday facts. Facts of why am I getting overdue bills in my name from companies I've never heard of, at age twelve and why are the English Setters now dead, next to their bowls without any signs of trauma. You might ask is it nature or nurture? Chalk up part of it to being born to a woman in the Depression who resented giving birth, and to a daughter, no less. It meant my grandmother had to give up her golf game and bridge. Plus, Mom was a difficult child. Pictures of her youth depict a young girl who never made eye contact. And she liked to play with fire. Once she left home and married Dad, they hopscotched across the country. That seemed to be the best way to deal with job loss and bills that couldn't be paid. Mom used to say that they moved thirty-two times in eleven years. She was proud of that. When we landed in NY and I started the third grade, I recited that fact to my teacher. When her mouth dropped open in astonishment, I realized that maybe it wasn't the badge of accomplishment I had always heard.

Trio

Fires three of which we knew, the first at twelve
the last one set at forty-two, before she came to Jesus.

                          The fires drew her to the flame.

Beauty of the heat, purifying sear of touch
before it was too much as everything melted,
returning to the core, what it was before
it all had to go away.

Incinerated, black-thick smoke,
fumes in the air

                      acrid ash
                                        mesmerized
                    the breeze

Dust-to-dust, arriving full-circle. Disappeared, at last.
And, no one found out. Only whispered blame.

Pyromania.

                      Mom.

Fires   three of which we knew

sparks of the devil
tell the truth from whence they came
                          only whispered blame

Ancestry

Half-brother of mine, found after a lifetime.
A full measure of family surrounds,
except the mom that you've been looking for.

Desire hollowed by the years,
yet eyes kept searching,
scouring pictures, faces in the crowds,
always asking why of the darkened silence.

        How do you let go of reaching for her clouds?
        Will you ever touch the moon again?
        Can you even swim in that Sea of Tranquility?

Oh, Todd, brother of mine, let's fly through the past together—
we'll hold hands, double-dog daring the did-you-knows
and whittling the what-ifs
to a promise. Of tomorrow.

Carpe Diem Meets Nana on Hollywood Blvd.

Wipe the film from your eyes. Turn from the routine,
the ho-hum seven-eleven existence of your life
spelled out in hum-drum schedules.
Toss it aside.

Don't you remember *Back to the Future*?
The f*cking clock is ticking.
Big Ben is looking, go ahead. I dare you. Call in sick.
Time to watch *Ferris Bueller's Day Off* again.

Go find the cracks the ants are crawling from.
What are those tree frogs croaking about?
Where are the waves endlessly breaking?
It can't be that far to Fiji, once you've been
On The Waterfront.

Those clouds are begging to be chased
in your *Field of Dreams*.
Be your own Humphrey Bogart, even Jimmy Stewart.
It's a Wonderful Life
even on *The African Queen*.

Elemental

Sweeter than August peaches
and just as ripe: a surprise in the mail.

The check came yesterday.
I sighed, realizing what that meant.
I'm too old to be doing this.

No, not a moment like Icarus
flying dangerously close to the sun—
but I did come nearer to a meltdown
than I'd like.

Even Mark Twain had money problems.

Table for One

An invitation to explore, reserve the table
nothing more to disturb your viewing pleasure,
at the waterfront, no burden of conversation.

Hold your head high. Look the maitre'd in the eye
and say, a split of champagne, please.

The occasion is yours.
Focus first on the orchid's magenta, speckled in the vase.
Linen cloth covers teak, sterling gleams in the soft light.
The surface breaks, pulling your eyes away.

Sip your drink.

Main course, perhaps the filet blood-rare, or duck-Peking?
You decide, as you tuck tradition aside.
Do whatever feels right with the leftovers.

The other gals are looking
envy in their glances, romance wilted
before the lettuce, egos hide under their breath,
the yes-dears contemplate how to get even.

Table for one?
Thank your lucky stars and Venus, jeweled
in the evening sky.

More Likely than Watching Squirrel Sex

How to succeed as a writer:

Surrender first to your muse. Flirt with hedgerows
and highbrow urges,
but go for the gusto, make unmitigated messes.
Confess all over the page, then lick it up with a spoon.
Only you can know what it means, but the whole world
deserves a taste.

Embrace full-frontal—unlike the squirrels. Find the vellum
and the fancy quill pen.
Curlicues with a touch of whimsy help you figure it out
on the fly. Caress goodbyes.

Charge what it's worth.
In a million years there will be a thousand like you
so flaunt the original. Now.

Make them pay the price; it's a steal, a doozy of a deal,
compared to what you paid
to find those damned words, in the first place.

Some call it angst, hell, it's the Super Bowl of Greek tragedies.
Isn't that what makes poetry cathartic? And the reviews will say:

With searing syllables, uncanny nuance
and an aching vision we haven't seen
in decades, she artfully couples images
never before conceived.

Now let's get back to the squirrels.

Kung Fu Nuns of Kathmandu

I'm taking the Santa Claus napkins
to Saturday's picnic, mid-July.
Who's to say we'll get this time in December?

Let's pull the sky over us through Michelangelo's clouds
and sit back, for a lazy-susan Sunday complete
with blueberry pancakes and giggles from granddaughters.

I'll show them the Kung Fu Nuns of Kathmandu
where every Jigme takes the stage:
Fearless Ones with the swords, slashing misconceptions
like devil dragons, all around.

Why do we think nuns can't do this?

Don't let me be invisible, any longer
dismissed when retirement plans slip out
or mask ties tug on hearing aids. *Por Dios!*

May the magic of the Kung Fu Nuns of Kathmandu
take me, sword and all, to my own nirvana
and what I'll say next time I'm asked what I'm doing.
I'll chuckle, murmuring under my breath
about skinny-dipping after dark
while I wash blueberries and fold napkins.

Lawrence Ferlinghetti Says Goodbye

The world is a beautiful place to be born into,
a Coney Island of the mind, even with a bomb now and then
or the occasional accidental death like Prince's.

Back then, Minneapolis was known for his music, not its murders.

Mr. Williams was deliberate.
Check out, man, before the walker arrives
with the shower chair and mechanical soft meals
to prevent aspiration.
No choking allowed.

He freed himself from the failings of his mind.
Ahh
In a flash
Done-----Gone
Hanging----------------Hung

I miss you, Robin: gnarly nose, and lopsided grin
whirling monologues you gave
in a dervish-spinning style, even as the clock kept ticking....

Yes, this world is the best place of all
for making babies and goosing statues
even if in the middle comes
                        the smiling mortician

From My Caesura

Pack the picture with the grandkids,
feel the breeze prickle your skin,
wiggle toes in the fine black mica sand.
Shiver a little, as you *slouch towards Bethlehem*.

Stand tall on every rock: ascend Everest if you must.
Apollo, Zeus, even Jesus is waiting.

Show the troika what you've got
as seconds count the minutes and hours fillet the weeks
in this year of your life, a crucible you cannot forget.

Build the retirement home you've always wanted
on American Express, that forever place
in the perfect *location, location, location*.

Count stars from the roof
pocketing the Milky Way in obsidian darkness.

Touch the bones of every dream.

Acknowledgments

"A Time Like This" was first published *In the Quarantined Room* (Laura Riding Jackson Foundation, 2020).

My sincere thanks go to Ms.Sally Naylor, who has been my coach and guide through this process. Her expertise has been invaluable.

Thanks to my fellow writers in the Porch Poets group, who have read and critiqued most of the entries.

And, finally, hats off to Skipwith Coale, who's not only been my co-leader in the Porch Poets, but reviewed the manuscript and gave me timely suggestions. Thanks, Skip!

Praise for *After Pyre*

In *After Pyre*, her second collection of poetry, P.M. Draper skillfully and piercingly explores what it means to experience both personal and collective trauma. Written in radiant, unfancy language, her poems speak of family dysfunction and tragedy, the pandemic, illness and ageing—all with bracing clear-sightedness and compassion, defiance, abundant humor, and above all, an abiding sense of hope. Draper's poetry asks difficult questions: how does one move through the world while haunted by memories of violent sibling deaths, mental illness, addiction? How does one find beauty and joy amidst enormous suffering and loss? These galvanizing poems implore and inspire the reader to embrace possibility in the face of heartache. They are a stunning testament that, out of chaos and ruin, we humans are endlessly capable of discovering the power to live fully, *to touch the bones of every dream.*

—Skipwith Coale

PM Draper's music is slant, whimsical and deeply satisfying. In the first stanza of "Illuminati," she juxtaposes Amsterdam, Bangkok, and Vienna, employs personification, auditory imagery, nouns used as verbs, several cliches, and alliteration. She wakes her reader and then employs the ancient trope: apostrophe, before we're swept to Tierra del Fuego. She roams the page restlessly and yet paradoxically, seems at home in her country: poetry. You won't be the same after reading about squirrel sex or the "Kung Fu Nuns of Kathmandu."

—Sally Naylor, author of *Synapse into Startle*

About the Author

P.M. Draper is a baby-boomer who retired during the pandemic. Her previous book of verse, *The Tao of Hibiscus* was published in 2020. She won 2nd place in the Covid competition for her poem "A Time Like This" which appears here in *After Pyre*. She's been a closet-poet for years, coming out in 2018 when she joined a local writers' group. She lives in Vero Beach, Fl with her husband and Boston Terrier, Oreo.

About The Poetry Box®

The Poetry Box, a boutique publishing company in Portland, Oregon, provides a platform for both established and emerging poets to share their words with the world through beautiful printed books and chapbooks.

Feel free to visit the online bookstore (thePoetryBox.com), where you'll find more titles including:

Synapse Flies into Startle by Sally Naylor

In the Jaguar's House by Debbie Hall

Dear John— by Laura LeHew

The Weight of Clouds by Cathy Cain

Let's Hear It For the Horses by Tricia Knoll

Of the Forest by Linda Ferguson

What We Bring Home by Susan Coultrap-McQuin

The Catalog of Small Contentments by Carolyn Martin

Tell Her Yes by Ann Farley

Moroccan Holiday by Lauren Tivey

Late Fall Bucolics by Anne Coray

Contraband by Juan Pablo Mobili

Olympic by John L. Miller

and more . . .

www.ingramcontent.com/pod-product-compliance
Lightning Source LLC
LaVergne TN
LVHW012131070526
838202LV00056B/5952